MELE

MELE
by Kalehua Kim

Copyright © July 1, 2025 Kalehua Kim

No part of this book may be used or performed without written consent of the author, if living, except for critical articles or reviews.

Kim, Kalehua
1st edition

ISBN: 978-1-949487-36-7
Library of Congress Control Number: 9781949487367

Interior design by Natasha Kane
Cover design by Joel W. Coggins
Author photo by Shirley Cai
Editing by Denise Low and Kris Bigalk

Trio House Press, Inc.
Minneapolis
www.triohousepress.org

To my mother, for this voice.
To my brothers, for their memories.
To my husband, for always listening.
To my children, for singing their own songs.

Kāhea

Ka Hale, The Nurturing Place
A mele for my mother

Come and read to me tonight.
I have lost all but one tale
you told to me in childhood.
Days were longer then,
as we grew together.
When tales were learned
not loved.
We were alone in your empty house
Ka Hale, the house of the bower.

Come and sing to me tonight.
Place me gently on your bed of moss
as midnight words
flicker into dawn.
Kuhi no ka lima – your hands tell the story.
As I mimic each gesture
your voice raises in chant,
sweeter than virgin tongue.
Lift your stories from my ear
to fill this house, *Ka Hale*.
Embrace me in your scarves,
your hinahina moss,
bathe me in laua'e,
the leaves drenched with rain
from the mountainside,
so I may swim within
a rainbow. Show me
how green we can be,
pressing ti shoots into the ground
together, packing down moist earth.

One day your voice will become mine,
Ka leo o maua.
Though I am not prepared for your end

to signal my beginning,
you urge me to remain
standing upon the cool, green moss.
Until I learn your words,
house me in your colors,
Ka Hale.

Table of Contents

Kāhea

Ka Hale, The Nurturing Place   3

ʻEkahi

A Heart (In)Action   13
Little heart   15
Dying looks like   17
After Her Funeral, I Dream That My Mother Tells Me Her Dreams   18
Good Daughter   19
Ghosts/ʻUhane   20
Glottal Stop : My Mother's Last Words   22
My Mother and I Speak Through the Pendulum   24
KS Class of '57   25
Impression   26
Telephone Suite   27
Not One Parking Space   29
When I am homesick   30

ʻElua

Beetmilk   35
Company   36
Reunited   38
Memory Sonnet   40
My Father's Sonnet   41
My Mother's Sonnet   42
Woman's Work   43
Domestication   44
Unwell   45
The First Test   46
Old Habits   47

Makaliʻi and the Stars That Followed	49
Fortune Cookie	50
Brooding	51
Offspring	52
We Fall	54
Hā	55
After Everything	56
The Joy of Raising Chickens	58
How to Ground Yourself (After Couples' Therapy)	60
Keloid	61
Songs for the Life I Chose or How to Stay Together	62
Inosculation	64
My Mother's Voice Echoes with Mine	65

Haʻina   67

Haʻina Hou

Seated Beside Happiness	81
Notes	83
Mahalo piha	87
About the Author	91

'Ekahi

A Heart (In)Action

Today someone sings about a broken heart.
Tomorrow I could sing about a broken heart.

The song on the radio can't tear me like tissue
the way your grunts and groans shred my heart.

I hold your hand that can no longer hold mine.
Pressure builds, forces the chambers of my heart

to implode with a rush of feeling, a gush without a gash.
My ribs splay open, jagged fingers reaching for a heart

just out of reach. My lungs expand and contract
too quickly, a red balloon stretched thin, a heart

deflated and limp on the ground, still tethered to
a white ribbon around my wrist where some heart

pulses, beats a frantic rhythm against my skin.
How can you mend a broken heart?

The hospice nurse says your pulse is slow,
your organs are shutting down. Your heart

is taking in less blood, pushing out less oxygen.
Although you are silent now, I hear your heart

rattle and clang like the Big Ben alarm clock
you wound each night before bed, its heart

an intricate puzzle of gears whose wheels
entwined like fingers before springing a heart

into action. I have no key to wind. No way to
revive you. I can barely gather my own heart's

implosion, the shattered shards of my ribs will
never fit the same way around this damaged heart.

How can I, your only daughter, mend anything?
How can I, your only daughter, be mended?

Little heart,

       fist-sized,

             thrice-humped instead of two.

It blooms a sacred tulip, opens

                the hand of a child's drawing.

You'd think it would grow

           smaller and smaller

as I pinch pieces of it off for you,

               dig my thumbnail into it

to cut away the blood and sinew,

             to pop juicy morsels into your

mouth.

        It's more

                  like the arm of the
            starfish,

         tail of the gecko,

slices of sea cucumber strewn on the ocean floor,

               waiting to multiply.

While you sleep

       I trace the red whorls

				stained into my fingertips

counting days

				counting beats.

Dying looks like

a white porcelain cup delivered to your table,
spirits rising like steam. It doesn't matter who
places it there, careful of your elbows and cutlery.
A well-intentioned mourner sits so long beside you
it's impossible to take a sip without being rude
(even at this late hour you will remember your manners).

The well-intentioned arrive every hour, relieve one
another with little relief for you, or those you'd prefer
to have gathered around your bed. They squeeze your
hand then wring their own. Damp tissues spill from
their sweater sleeves, crushed petals under the hospital bed.

You yearn for the days when your people died
in the beds in which they were born.
Generations depressing metal bedsprings,
comforted against the dark, pushed into the light.

You remember white sheets embroidered with tiny blue
flowers, a jagged seed stitch worn and discolored
from the nights you lay awake in the dark,

the cotton weave a balm against the night air.
You would pull the blankets to your chest,

rub each petal between thumb and forefinger until the cold came in.

After Her Funeral, I Dream That My Mother Tells Me Her Dreams

My maddah came to me at da end –
so many times she came –
we would sit, all quiet

at da small kine table
in her kitchen –
but you know

she wanted fo' sit at da window, yah?
Wanted fo' watch da
light on da mountain,

wanted fo' watch you
kids in da yahd,
playing in da grass,

hiding between da trees
fo' sneak up on da horses.
But da horses, dey

could smell you kids comin',
you nevah fool dem,
jus like I nevah fool her.

My maddah, she came so quiet,
she nevah have to say notin'.
She jus wait, she wait fo' me, yah?

An I goin' wait da same kine.
I goin' be like da horses.
I goin' wait fo' you.

Good Daughter
> *After Franny Choi*

Washed the dishes; mopped the floors; smiled
for the photos; aced the test; passed two more;
mixed the batter smooth; frosted; read the cards

right; played the cards right; recited the directions;
eased the tension; dealt everyone a fair hand;
collected; wore hose and sensible shoes; chest out

shoulders back; looked both ways; bloomed;
waved on; composed; complimented; complied;
crossed; dipped the nib deep; pressed hard

to open the tip; darkened the ink; etched thick
lines across the body; pricked the pulp;
bled the deckled edges; smeared; stabbed

the crease; stitched each signature; carved
a cover; bound the words to skin; cleaved.

Ghosts / 'Uhane
After Kiki Petrosino and Anne Sexton

All ghosts are my mother

                                        All 'uhane are my mother

    neither angry nor sad,

    hair curled and lipstick bright

Not witches, but ghosts

                                  'A'ole nā ho'okalakupua, akā nā 'uhane

    leaving slippers by the door,

    welcome guests who kiss my cheek.

Not all ghosts will mother.

                                  Not all 'uhane will mother.

    Others may sing, but not with her voice.

    They come to me not as mothers, but as stories.

                            'A'ole lākou i hele mai ia'u ma ke 'ano
                                he makuahine, akā, he mo'olelo.

    They are a shifted, tumbled type

    that I ache to press into my skin.

                              But that isn't all.

Some ghosts are birds.

                                Some ghosts are manu kama'āina.

    Neither plumed nor beaked,

  feet as sharp as barbed wire

Not angels, but birds

                  'A'ole nā 'ānela, akā, nā manu

  they run toward the sky

  knowing there is no heaven.

Glottal Stop : My Mother's Last Words

the words you taught
me sit always under
the surface,

mama

with breath in
song sung out
breath against
the inside of
my mouth,

mama

we shared so
many words
all we didn't say

full
before
the glottal stop

uh uh
uh uh

the open juncture
the obstructed breath
I don't remember
if your eyes opened

but the stop between
breaths
the tone in
the tune out

uh uh

still nestled
within the closure
of the throat

My Mother and I Speak Through the Pendulum

    If you need me to say it, *Yes*.
It was wrong of me to think you knew.

                                  If you need me to hear it, *Yes*.
                                      I will try to believe that, too.

If you need me to see it, *Yes*.
  I see your arms open, true.

                                  If you need me to feel it, *Yes*.
                                    You are all around me, proof.

KS Class of '57

You look crisp and ready.

You sit upright in your graduation photo, a cool collar at your neck, pressed as tight as your smile. I never noticed that dimple before, but I watched you draw on those eyebrows every day of my young life, rapt at the woman in the mirror – she's the one I watched while you put your face on every day. She sat at the dressing table in her bra and panties following the same routine as each dark morning dawned: moisturizer, concealer under the eyes, foundation, powder to set. Then green matte eye shadow, black liquid eyeliner (always dot the beauty mark), black mascara, blush. You'd wait until you had breakfast before lining your lips and applying lipstick.

The woman in the mirror focused intently on the woman in the mirror. Their deft fingers, the critical eye they fixed on one another made me feel like an outsider. I gazed at a woman in the eyes of a woman. We all, we each, becoming women. Becoming something someone somewhere decided was a woman.

Were you ready, Judith? Did you hold your slender neck just so, look directly into the photographer's lens and think, "I have arrived?" Are those two points of light in your eyes the camera's light bouncing back an answer for you?

When I look in the mirror I see the tall slope of your forehead. People said we looked alike, but we never agreed. But I do have something of yours reflecting back at me, something broad and brown and painted on my face.

Impression

Every morning my mother painted on red lips:
Wine with Everything, Fire and Ice, Really Red lips.

I woke to kisses blotted all over my face,
little love songs at my temple, on my forehead, lips.

They seeped under my skin, but it still took time to learn
her songs when I sang through my cracked lips.

She could sing all night without dulling a point
in her Cupid's bow, soft notes from tinted lips.

My father grew tired of her voice. My brothers couldn't
match her pitch, couldn't follow with their misted lips.

So I carried her kisses, took her songs into my bones.
I will always be marked by her – now dead – lips.

I pluck a tube from her dressing table: Lehua Blossom.
I gather her sheet music, where I press my newly painted lips.

Telephone Suite

*

I don't remember her name but in my mind I see her green floral-patterned polyester pantsuit and her sharp, shark nose jutting from her face, her heavy-framed gray plastic glasses with smudged lenses clouding her steely gray eyes. I remember her gray hair – more dirty dark dishwater than silver – parted in the middle, standing at attention at her shoulders. I remember her black stacked-heel open-toed sandals clacking against the linoleum when she walked from her cubicle to my mother's in their small office. I remember all of this but especially her voice, a tiny gravel at the back of her throat scraping the tender shell of my ear through the cream-colored receiver against my chin as I lay in my parents' bed, the green pastoral bedspread always a comfort even if the pillow shams felt too silky on my cheek. I believe she thought herself gentle on that hot August morning when she woke me from a deep teenage sleep. I don't believe I will ever forget her voice through the telephone line, rough and shimmied through the receiver's little black holes, shaving a crease now embedded in my cartilage, transforming a whorl in the chamber. I don't believe she'd ever even been to our house before she rubbed that rock rough and ready, tearing green leaves off the bed to chafe inside my ear: *Your mother's coming to get you because your father is dead.*

*

In the hospital basement on a pay phone another mouthpiece against my chin, the coiled silver cord in my opposite hand, already damp from my sweaty palm, I had to tell him, me at 13 and he at 19 at college, probably hung over and pissed that his little sister had woken him to give him this crap news, this little sister who called to tell him something sad, something awful, something that would change our lives forever, this little sister who called because that's what family does, this little sister who gave him sad news but who really needed to be given comfort, this little sister standing at the pay phone bank in the basement of the hospital holding a chipped, cracked, black receiver alone under harsh fluorescent tube lights so sure of what to do, but unsure of what comes next. In the years after, my mother would ask *have you talked to your little brother?* and I didn't understand why but when I think of that time in the hospital basement I know that I was the bearer of a great weight that I heaved over my shoulder, a weight that displaced me from my brother and I imagine that in my mother's eyes perhaps the carrying of a weight like that might make me stronger than simply being someone's little anything.

*

Then, years later the call that I expected, the call that I knew would come for me. I was in bed again but this time waking to my brother's voice. It wasn't you that came for me, Mother, it wasn't your voice beckoning me from a dream or your lips at my temple, soft song in my ear. It was the electronic bleat of the hotel's flat-handled landline, echoing before sunrise my brother's gentle voice, rasping, *we want to have time with her before the funeral home people get there.* I understood his immediacy. I was slow to get out of bed. I sat up, blinking into this strange silence. All I wanted was your voice in my head, not the image of a stranger in a green floral-patterned polyester pantsuit delivering the message that you should have given me yourself. Or my brother in a hotel room down the hall, shouldering a phone to his ear, buttoning up an aloha shirt but most likely still in sleep shorts. I always thought you would come to me, Mother. That the great grave grip of your voice tethered to the long-coiled lines of my gut would sing me into knowing. But you died in a hospital bed instead of in my dreams. I felt powerless without that weight. I couldn't remember when you last ate but I remember that the pink pajamas I wanted to dress you in were already soiled. We had been sitting with you all week, bathing you, changing you. We had been waiting for this moment. How could I stand when my world shifted so silently? I pulled the sheets back, placed one foot on the hotel carpet. Then the other. The room spun green. The world had been spinning all this time. It's still spinning.

Not One Parking Space

I have come home to Hawaiʻi and my mother is silent,
no slamming screen door, no bird poop on my shoulder,
no walking into spiderwebs. Not one parking space.

I stand in my mother's childhood home,
hearing only echoes of the living.
I sit in her chair at the table, but it is cold.

How can she find me, left at sea,
her ashes water-logged,
soaked and salted on the ocean floor?

Or is she floating still, lighter than limu,
rippling and waving, reflecting blue
mercury on the surface of the open water?

Other mothers find me here:
my aunts, my stepmother, my sister-in-law's mother,
even my nieces, who mother their own children now,

they all come to me, mothers mothering me.
Mothering with a silence that is not her silence. Not doors,
not birds, not webs. Not one parking space.

When I am homesick

he brings me mangoes   lines them up on the counter   waits while I pick   the last one has an asymmetrical hump   I find appealing   deep blush of orange on its face   heft right in my hand   I press it to my mouth   I smell her   the allure of my mother   I roll the mango over my face   we are cheek to cheek   my mother and me   oh, the ripeness of memory   I roll the mango across my forehead   I kiss its tough smooth skin   I roll it down my chin to the opposite temple   she is verdant   this mother   she vibrates against my palms   I hold her in both hands   a sodden seed   I carry   that is all she asked of me   I press the mango to the center of my chest   *this is how I hold you   now*

'Elua

Beetmilk

And what if the screams had turned to laughter?
After three sons the dream of a girl's laughter

out of the womb was reason enough to keep trying.
My mother preened nightly despite her sons' laughter.

Before bed she hid her seeds in the sugar bowl,
brought in weeds from the garden, her laughter

shaking the beads of dew from her dandelions. She
ironed white rags, seams suppressing wrinkled laughter.

She folded the starched corners neatly into ovals,
placed the sweet orbs under her bed, where laughter

rarely ruffled the cotton sheets: him politely on top. The
boys helped, pulled beets long enough to stop their laughter,

their hands dancing red bird feet onto her belly. She
cooked naked, the beet greens braised in heated laughter,

their wilted veins retreating under brown sugar.
She (and I) grew, bellies bursting without laughter.

My mother counted the days pleating paper fans.
Inside, I bounced to the beat of my brothers' laughter.

When my mother's reams of paper ran out, it was time to
collect her hidden seeds from the sugar bowl. Her laughter

bubbled over – she had succeeded in turning them to milk.
She knew there would be no bleeding today, but laughter?

I landed in the garden weeds, a red-fingered flower
without a stem. My greedy mouth open, opening for laughter.

Company

Try come, bebe,
Aunty not goin' hurt you.
Cannot make it bettah if you no come by
Oooooo, so beeg you came!
Yo' ahms stay looonngg an yo' lehgs stay groen!
Come, come sit by Aunty. Lemme touch yo' hed, bebe.
Aunty jus goin' touch, sof-kine, see? No hurt.
Hea. Feel dis leef.
Cool, yah?
Goin' make yo' hed cool an sof,
goin' be mo' bettah.
Goin' help you sleep,
goin' make all da scah go down.
Yah, das righ, sit with Aunty lil wile.
Aunty jus take da leef, put hea on yo' hed.
Bettah, yah?
Den we wrap on da bandanna—
I tot you like da peenk one—
jus goin' tie um in da back.
Les jus sit togeddah, we talk story.
Bumbai Aunty sing a song, but fo' now goin' talk story.
Bout a beudeeful girl who wen bump her hed, jus like you.
Da girl, Florence, wen walking in da fores.
Wanted fo' peek flowah fo' make lei, yah?
But wen she wen reach up to da high tree, she fell.
Bump her hed on da way down.
She cry, oh she cry! She not so brave like you.
She cry until her maddah come.
Deh take her to da beeg house, wipe up her teahs and da blood.
Still, she cry.
Her maddah rock her, quiet.
Her maddah put da leef on her hed, wrap um up
an dey rock
an dey sleep.
Do dat each nigh until all bettah.

Jus one small scah, no can see um anymoah.
She cannot even feel um wid her ruff kine hands.
Das righ, jus relax, bebe. Aunty stay wid you.
Oh, you can feel dat? Jus one small scah now, yah?
Yo' hans stay cold, bebe, les put da blanket on top.
Yah, I hold my han on yo' foahed
an you keep yos on mine.
We keep company, yah?

Reunited

The strike of the match against
the matchbox fumes, stinks
as Carolyn leans in, right hand cradles
the now flaming match head
beneath the burner,
left hand controlling the
click-click-click-click
of the gas. *Foom.* It takes.
She will brown the meat, drain
the oil, then add sauce.
Nicole and I sing Peaches and Herb
sitting at the long, green table.
The perspiration under our thighs
glues us to the bench.

Reunited and it feels so gooooood,

Nicole tries to hold the note as long
and loud as she can, her breath vibrating
until Aunty Florence calls from the porch,

Kuli kuli! You goin' wake up Tūtū!

Nicole stops immediately.
I don't even giggle and Carolyn attempts
to hush the meat sizzling in the pan.
We are quiet for almost a minute.
I watch the thin, red hand on the clock
start on the 4 and no one moves
until it reaches the 11.
I sneeze when it touches the 2.
Softly, slowly, I whisper,

Reeeunited, cause we understoooodd,

and Nicole, forgetting Tūtū
stands up, bellows,

    There's just ONE PEEERRRFFEECCT TH---

And before she finishes the word, 'thing,'
A smeared white image appears
at the corner of my eye.
It walks slowly – drifts, really –
to the dead brown bananas that
hang in the back corner of the kitchen.
A whitish hand grabs the fly swatter
next to them, drifts to Nicole.
We watch the fly swatter, clutched
in Tūtū's ghostly hand,
hit Nicole on her okole,

    Thwack!

Nicole sits. Tūtū drifts back to the
corner, replaces the fly swatter,
opens the screen door and walks out.
Only the meat replies,
Aunty's voice echoing from the porch,

    I told you.

Memory Sonnet

Although I have come back for the summer,
my father's house has never been my home.
His silence, humid and thick as thunder,
hangs heavier than the sun-sapped mangoes
outside my window, their dense, orange flesh
sweating sugar, needing conversation.
When I ask him what he remembers best
about meeting my mother, his smile beams,
revealing more than one of his dimples.
He says, "We met at da bus company."
Something so benign, something so simple,
I'm surprised when he goes on suddenly,
"She used to sing, yah? Ho, da voice she got,
in da house, in my hed, an in my haht."

My Father's Sonnet

All da drivahs on da buses knew yo' maddah.
She worked da desk, yah? Whea dey check in,
an she was attractive, so we knew her.
I remembah yo' Uncle George, I remembah
him from City an County, an I knew she
was George's sistah. So was easy fo' talk to her.
I wen ask her out fas' kine, I nevah like nobody
go out wid her but me. I cannot remembah
whea we went, maybe bumbai we went fo'
drinks or someten', was long time.
Yah, she used to sing. All da time, me an
yo' braddahs would hea her. Bumbai, I couldn't
tink fo' her voice all ovah da place.
In da house, in my hed, in my haht.

My Mother's Sonnet

Your father said he wanted to be free.
The boys were pitching tents in the back yard,
setting down stakes, building kingdoms in trees.
You were there, wearing a green leotard,
princess slippers, with a tutu in hand.
He and I sat at the dining table
where I fidgeted with my wedding band,
where he rewrote our family fable.
I want to be free. I heard him say it
again and again in my mind – it took
me years to understand, then to admit
that marriage wasn't like a story book,
an easy tale where the prince becomes king.
It's a harmony I hope you can sing.

Woman's Work

An apron will not keep you
from becoming soiled.
Its crisp creases fool no one.
Examine it closely for stains:
A splatter of marinara,
burnt sugar crusted on the hem,
the blood of beets.
No cloth can keep you clean,
and the ties will dig into your flesh,
taut as butcher's twine.
Sitting in the dark will not help you,
no matter how many peas you shell,
their hollow skins in a heap on your lap
as you struggle to fill an empty bowl.

Domestication

I might want to fold him up neatly. Tuck in any errant sleeves, fold him into thirds with crisp lines and flatten him by the neck. He would fit so nicely into the dresser drawer. If I were feeling very ambitious, I would employ tidy tricks by Marie Kondo, fold him into lengthy rectangles until he is smaller than a pocket square, standing at attention whenever I open the drawer. I would color code him, light to dark, days of levity in the front for easy reach, growing darker as the drawer goes deep, where I might reach in with a long arm and a grimace on my face to deal with the color run in the wash. I would stop using dryer sheets with contaminating phthalates. I would only use the gentlest cycle, laundry flakes reserved for intimates and infants. I would take good care of him, yes, and he would remain pressed in with all the other lovers I've stacked – the cowl necked sweaters, the sweats with missing drawstrings, the yellow-stained undershirts, the bras with misshapen underwire that dig into my side boob. He would be the most presentable of all my outfits, even sweeter than the LBD in the back of the closet. He would be the long hang, the French cuffed blouson draped trench saved for special occasions.

Unwell

After we made love I cried
a flood into the crook of his neck.
I wanted to be so close to him, be a part
of him finally, help his skin melt away into mine
so we were no longer two people, but one
steady rhythm. A rhythm beating toward a
common release, a common dream.

I cried after loving him in the past.
Had counted on its blessed wetness on my
face. The low tone of his voice could make
my eyes water, pull the well up from inside
in an overwhelming need to empty myself
so I could love him
again.

The First Test

During the drive home I took the yam out of my purse and tucked
it into the waistband of my pants, with scratches, marks, roots still

hanging on. In the store, I had four items in my basket: a small bag
of chips, Sofia Coppola wine in a can, the yam, and the test. I ate

the chips while waiting to pay, stuffed the items into my purse and
walked to the store's restroom. Inside, I popped the can top, gulped

the wine down, relieved by the cool burn at my throat. I placed
the can gently onto the bed of used paper towels in the trashcan and

turned my attention to the test. I was surprised at the amount of
space in the box; the test took up just a small corner and the directions

were folded neatly around it. I read the five steps of the "How to Use"
portion. Read them again. I peeled open the packet slowly so as

not to accidentally drop the test stick, then laid the wrapper next to
the wine can. During the two-minute wait I tried to clear my mind

and think of the yam. *A yam has hard skin.* I closed my eyes.
Because it has to twist down into the dirt to get what it needs.

Old Habits

Aunty Florence and Tūtū sit at the long
green table, shelling boiled peanuts.
"Da bebe goin' come soon," Aunty says.
Tūtū separates the darker, thin, inner
shell liner from the meat. "Mmm."

"Tonight," Aunty says without looking
up as she tosses a wrinkled shell
into the plastic bowl between them,
a soft thud. Aunty peels seven, eight,
nine more peanuts before looking at Tūtū.

Tūtū's circle of peanuts grows almost
as wide as the plastic bowl between them —
moist, misshapen mounds with spines
down the center where once they fused
together, then split apart, some while still
in their silent sacs on the vine, others
slit by the gnarled brown thumb of an
old ghost woman who has given up tarot
cards and ti leaves for good, but keeps her
white cotton nightgown and straggled bits
of tweeded hair amass for effect or old faith.

"Wait," Tūtū looks directly into Aunty's face,
her pupils wide, black moons reflected
in clouded blue waters. "Soon."

Aunty Florence looks away first, looks down,
studies the circle of peanuts Tūtū makes,
only now notices they all face upwards,
curved vessels open, lying on their backs
with spines supporting their bodies to receive.

Aunty smiles. "I thought you quit."
"Ah," Tūtū says,
"Habit."

Makaliʻi and the Stars That Followed

It was a net of stars I struggled to lift,
my belly ready to spill its light.

My belly ready to spill its light,
I tipped like a cup, ready for release.

I tipped like a cup, ready for release,
ready to see the crown of my child's head.

Ready to see the crown of my child's head,
like the cluster of stars I saw months before.

The cluster of stars I saw months before
did not prepare me for the long, dark wait.

Not prepared for more longing or darkness,
I pushed until I broke open with light.

I pushed until my child broke into flight,
a net of stars that I struggled to gift.

Fortune Cookie
Your winsome smile will be your sure protection

I had the fortune
in my wallet, the black print
a scar on the clear plastic window
where my license is supposed to show.
It's practically the only thing that
kept me smiling –
not the baby at my breast
or the job I quit to take care of the baby,
and not Suesan, who told me,
Finally! Your ovaries made use of themselves!
The painful stretch of my lips,
barely allowing teeth to show,
only enacted at the thought of
that tiny strip of paper
when my mother-in-law asked,
Aren't you so happy now?
as she patted the fasteners on the baby's diaper,
refusing to hand her over after a change.

I smiled so hard my lips cracked,
the tiny fissures burning as I
fought to stay intact,
applying Aquaphor and Vaseline
and even once A&D diaper ointment
to keep it up, keep it together.

When my husband's lover
brought a gift for the baby,
my cheeks curved instantly,
a huge intake of air
followed by a wide smile,
teeth glaring in the sunlight
as I sang silently to myself,
Protect me, protect me.

Brooding

The egg is silent.
Hunched over the mottled shell,
the mother hen pecks and pecks,
sharp jabs to the top until a
fissure zig zags down its edge,
breaking open on the last pointed stab.

The mother pries the shell open,
frantic feathers plume around her
large eyes, beak poking.

The egg is empty.

Some aqueous fluid leaks
out, dribbles onto the twigs of
the nest, drips into a puddle.
But imagine instead a bowl by the stove
before breakfast is scrambled,
yellow with the hope of freshly
cracked eggs, yolks vibrant, thicker
and brighter than a mother's tears.

Offspring

Instead of eggs
I left with a fist
full of feathers.

Down sifted through
my fingers as I
fed my daughters,
who cooed gently,
turning their heads
from side to side
while the sun revealed
a grave iridescence
on their necks.

When their claws scratched
at the skin on my arms
I held them
closer to the sky.

When their beaks
pecked at my heart,
I clasped my hands
together to keep the
blood from flowing
over their combs.

When they molted,
I tucked them under
my arms, protecting
their wings tight
against my torso
until every barbule hooked.

I trod heavy steps
under their buoyance.

One day all they left behind
was a whistle of bones
and a flourish of feathers.

I never blinked an eye.

We Fall

We   are all birds   tiny birds   first birds   first   wet down   wet open mouth   blind   we wait   we wait   we hunger   we wait listen   call   caw   trill   thrum   rise wind   first wind   wet wing   wait   wet   wind wet wing   trill   no egg tooth   no tooth   no egg   first wet down   first wet tooth   first   wet   first wet wing   first tooth   call the river   call the rain   caw   we are all tiny mouths   caw   we are all blind   trill   we all wait   caw   we all hunger   listen   we thrum   we rise without wind   we weather without teeth   wait   wait for egg   wait for down   feather thrum   fall

Hā

when I was born I was a girl
I was a girl with a cord wrapped around my neck
I had a cord wrapped around my neck and no breath
I had no breath because until that moment, no one had hit me
no one had hit me and it took time to unravel the cord
it took time to unravel the cord but I feel its weight every day
every day there is a weight, although its source changes
the source changes because matter changes
matter changes by transforming molecules
molecules are in constant motion
the constant motion of children, whose voices echo
children's voices echo across canyons, leap from cliffs
we leap from cliffs when we stretch to seek balance
we stretch, balancing the past behind us and the future ahead
the past of us and the future crawl across an x axis
crawling across an x axis is only one way to look at time
the only way to look at time is to refuse to see time
to refuse time is to refuse everything you ever felt wrapped around your neck
unwrap the cord around your neck
unwrap the time it takes to catch your breath
catch your breath
catch your breath
that is your voice

After Everything

He wanted my name.
He wanted me to give it freely.
Color and light,
spores that spawn
fields of flowers,
my name is wild –
a dream that haunts
in a riot of hooves –
my name is an explosion
on the vine,
pepper to the retina.

He wanted my name
and I gave part of it to him,
flat as a brass plate
on a corner of the desk;
a tarnished band
around my finger.

But I did not offer him my song, Mother.
I held my breath.
I held my tongue.
I held my children
so tight that they
flew blindly.

When I sing to him
he will be unable to turn away.
My song will lick his lips
and leave nectar
at the back of his throat.
My song will singe
the dimple in his chin,
leave him panting
as he rounds out the vowels.

When I sing my song to him,
his eyes will seek mine
in a crowded room and
he will want nothing else
for days, will whisper me for weeks,
mumble me, mumble me, mumble.

I protected him from this –
hummed half-hearted harmonies
leaving him to doubt
the depth of my range,
my cadence,
my control.

But I will build my breath, Mother.
I will tongue a timbre that cements
siliceous lyrics into the shell of his ear.
I will revel in my expansion,
every vowel a crystalized chorus
ringing in woody resonance.

He and I will vibrate
long after the string of notes
dusts our feet like stars.

The Joy of Raising Chickens

Pointed feathers
fumble on pointed feet,

with wings that ripple
in the wind without lift.

They slip on sheets of moss,
bounding toward me,

beaded eyes glassine
against the morning.

Darling, downy dragons
that peck at my knees,

claw at my elbows,
perch on the round of my shoulder:

What is it to flap at the world
without finding flight?

Their soft scales
shine like river stones

pulling light from the
water's surface with each

refracted ripple.
If I toss them into the air,

how often would they skim
the surface to the opposite bank

or sink under the weight
of flight? If I push my pen

across this page, would
the letters leap

or bleed into my fingertips, heavy
and dark as my mother's whetstone?

How to Ground Yourself (After Couples' Therapy)

Rub the stone in your pocket. Wiggle your toes in your socks. Rinse the rice. Breathe in – think about mermaid hair – breathe out. Click the button on the rice pot. Eat burnt toast. Watch the curls of smoke from the toaster rise into the air. See something (smoke). Say something ("Fire!"). Remain calm as family members run into the room. Feel warm that loved ones came running when you yelled. Rub the stone again when they file out. Tease a crumb of toast from between your first and second molar with your tongue. Spread your hands on the floor as you go to hands and knees. Breathe out – cat – breathe in – cow. Listen to the thrum of a hummingbird's wings outside. Let go of the stone. *thhhhhrrruuummm.* Swallow the last bit of burn. *thhhhhrrruuummm.* Take a life from the cat. Moo because in your new life you are a cow. Press your palms into the stones arranged under your hands. *thhhhhrrruuummm.* Rinse each grain of rice from your spine. Glory in the mermaid hair flowing down your back. Wiggle your toes. Flutter iridescent wings behind your eyelids.

Sing, "I am _____," even if you sing it softly. *thhhhhrrruuummm.*

thhhhhrrruuummm.

Keloid

When love is a kind of trauma, I run toward the hurt.
I kneel at the wing of Eros and hook myself with slick barbules.
I thrive on this metal, take it with my morning fiber and feel satisfied.
But the wound, the open hole and the blood, *that* surprises me!
The scab that dries out, itching incessantly until I must scratch.
Flakes of old skin leave my body to reveal its berry, fresh as flight.
Then the scar, the raised welt of purple – a comfort under my fingers,
the reminder of how deeply this desire marks me.
My lover kisses my scars and calls them valentine.
He laves his tongue over them like a cherry-flavored lozenge.
His tongue numbers them, hearts all over my body.
I grow myself around them, feel how they push against my organs.
I have never needed wings to ride the updraft.
Engorged, I savor my skin stretch.

Songs for the Life I Chose or How to Stay Together

*

A spring sun warms the vines we planted.
Heat emanates from the gravel –
an extra layer of protection.
Weed barrier, I whisper.
Weed barrier   weed barrier

*

I run the pad of my thumb over the large muscle
between his thumb and forefinger, gently
push forward until the full grape of him
is clasped in the V of me.

*

No spirit tastes as warm
as this spot. I relish its tilt.

*

The weight of fruit strengthens
the branch eventually. Just as synapses
electrify, endure memory.

*

I am surprised by the need to run
to him, straight from a summer shower,
skin damp, sweat dripping into my eyes.
No sunset, only this vintage.

*

The vines lose their leaves,
their flaming skirts clutching caps of acorns.
I braid him a wreath of red-tinged leaves,
fill our cups to toast the harvest –
my victor, my thimble.

*

The wind takes him away, carving a deep
silence in the snow. On the longest night
of the year, he returns, lays his palm upon the door
until I warm his branch-brittle fingers by the fire.
I lost my horse, he murmurs.

*

He weaves his song in my hair,
We are merrier   we are merrier
 we are merrier
his voice – spiced grape, gravel soft –
fresh as a foal in the hay.

*

He is here in our bed,
long-legged amidst the bud break.
His ripe skin warms me each dawn
when I cannot see the light
through the window, or my hands,
that find him deep in sleep. I hold on
there.

Inosculation
after Philemon and Baucis

we burrow
root to root
tap to lifeline
my leaves lobed
his broad hearts

we promise seedlings
tongue vines
between torsos
sip shoulders of moss

we swallow
tiny words
easier than air
our mingled mist
a deluge

guide light
we savor sun
guide root
we savor soil
guide green
we savor skin

in our moment
we breathe

My Mother's Voice Echoes with Mine

This is about you and me,	These voices that blend
mother and daughter,	hear them sing –
my gift to you –	hear them call
the most precious	songs of our lineage –
gift I give you –	a song for my daughters,
I've filled it with love,	a song for all our voices,
to help you understand who	sings the melody
I am and why you've become	the harmony we've become
every feeling,	every voice
a piece in the puzzle	between space and line,
of our relationship	without space without boundaries,
I don't know why some shine	high notes
and others dim but they do	ring in alternate registers –
It's the bright memories of our	oli oli oli –
life together that I've written	that echo

Haʻina

*

I tend my chickens like I tend my children. I feed them, clean up after them, hold them when they stand still long enough to sneak up behind them. I wonder if my mother ever felt this way. How do you hold them close without their claws ripping at your skin? How do you avoid a peck to the heart?

[My mother was born on an island]

*

The chickens run to the coop door, bodies low and squat, crowding wing to wing. They gather around me, peck at my boots. They hop up to the basket I'm holding, tear lettuce with their beaks, rip romaine from my fingers, leave green shards at my feet.

[same as her mother and her mother and me.]

*

My mother told me, *As a kid I hated going bathroom at night. We had to use the outhouse, take a kerosene lantern. There were always spiders, the webs stuck like one hair in your mouth. I thought my brothers would jump out at me, but it was usually just one chicken.*

[As a child she hid from bombs.]

*

The chickens come when I sing. Their crouched run across the grass is comical, endearing, even as one pecks at a freckle on my arm. What do they taste? I once dated a white guy who asked my mother for her mochiko chicken recipe. She didn't answer, just stared with beady brown eyes at the yard.

[As an adult she feared small spaces.]

*

I kept grandpa's shotgun on the shelf behind the bed. Of course I did! It was a good neighborhood, but you don't know, yah? I never shot it, but you'd be surprised how many times I caught your Aunty's boyfriend sneaking out. Good thing it wasn't loaded.

[Armed with only her songs,]

*

Every week we dance hula in my Aunty's garage, hapa-haole songs, mostly. The kāhiko is too hard on my mother's knees. She makes me sing along with the record.

Good thing she don't sing like one chicken, My mother cackles at my Aunty, swaying her hips, *Bumbai no catch one rooster!*

[she married, had children, he left her.]

*

The day Elvis died my mother danced on the white shag carpet, red toenails peeking from the pile, her feet twisting, shifting, lifting the cuffs of her denim bellbottoms.

I saw him at Aloha Stadium in that white leather jumpsuit. He could shake it!

[My mother was born on an island,]

*

She grimaces, I think in pain, but I'm not sure. I try to be gentle as I see her shoulders rise and tense. *Are you in pain?* I ask, turning her hand to expose the inside of her forearm. I hope that today one shot will be enough.

Nah, she grunts, *No more pain.* But her shoulders still, rise on a stuttered inhale while her eyebrows draw in. Her brown eyes stare out the window, unfocused.

[with a song on her lips and a dance in her step.]

*

I tend my chickens like I wanted to tend my mother. I wanted to feed her, but she could not swallow. I combed her hair as she lay dying. I held her hand, rubbed her feet, propped her to avoid bedsores. She turned her head when I sang, her breath a feather.

I no longer care about claws. I don't know what my heart tastes.

[Now her ashes are scattered at sea.]

Ha'ina Hou

Seated Beside Happiness
For my mother

Your husband emails me photos of his garden:
overexposed leaves, the orchids you transplanted, a tree in the courtyard,
always with your statue of Quan Yin.
He calls me every month or so – admittedly high –
marveling at hidden images he finds in the photos.

I remember when Quan Yin stood on an end table in our living room,
serene on her black lacquered pedestal, her skirts caught in perpetual
    motion.
Laughing Buddha watched her from the other side of the room.

As a child I chose to be seated beside him. I chose to be seated beside
    happiness.

You let me tug his long earlobes, rub his bare belly.
Quan Yin was lovely, mid-flight, unreachable –
she still reminds me of you.

It is no wonder your husband photographs her often, lens angled, light
    filtered.
When he makes pictures, he makes you over and over in every light he
    can distill.

I write poems. I write poems where I can touch you.
I pull your ear and you listen.
I rub your belly and you sing me home.

Notes

In 'Ōlelo Hawai'i, the word *mele* means, "song."

The structure of this collection borrows from song structure found in many Hawaiian songs or hulas. A *kāhea* is the call made by a dancer to signal the first lines of a verse for the chanter. *'Ekahi* means, "one," which I've used here to denote the first verse. *'Elua* means "two," or the second.

The *ha'ina*, or the last verse(s) of a song acts as a summary repeating the song's theme and sometimes offers the name of a person to whom the song is dedicated. *Ha'ina hou* asks to tell the story one more time.

It is with deep gratitude and humility that I offer my understanding of 'Ōlelo Hawai'i and Hawaiian Creole English. Any variations in usage or translation reflect my current understanding and access. It is my hope this knowledge will continue to grow.

*

"A Heart (In)Action" incorporates a line from the song "How Can You Mend a Broken Heart," written by Barry and Robin Gibb, released in 1971. Although the version by the Bee Gees is the first version of the song I ever heard, the cover version by Al Green is the one that plays in my head.

"Ghosts/'Uhane" is inspired by the poem "Ghosts," by Kiki Petrosino from *Witch Wife*, (Sarabande Books, 2017) which is a line-by-line response to the poem "Ghosts," by Anne Sexton.

"Good Daughter" is inspired by the poem "Bad Daughter," by Franny Choi from *Soft Science* (Alice James Books, 2019).

"Reunited" incorporates lines from the song "Reunited," written by Dino Fekaris and Freddie Perren, which was sung by the R&B duo Peaches & Herb, released by Polydor Records in 1979.

"Domestication" was inspired by a book review by Walter Kirn in *The New York Times* (Feb. 4, 2022). His review of *Foreverland, On the Divine Tedium of Marriage* by Heather Havrilesky suggested in the headline that "Heather Havrilesky Compares Her Husband to a Heap of Laundry."

"Makaliʻi and the Stars That Followed" is a duplex, a form created by poet Jericho Brown. Makaliʻi is the Hawaiian name of the cluster of stars commonly known as the Pleiades. For Hawaiians, its rising signals a new year and a change of seasonal weather patterns.

"Hā" can be translated from Hawaiian as "the breath of life." This poem was chosen by Heid E. Erdrich as a winner of the 2023 James Welch Prize for Indigenous Poetry.

"Songs for the Life I Chose or How to Stay Together" was inspired by the poem "Songs from the House of Death, Or How to Make It Through to the End of a Relationship" by Joy Harjo from *A Map to the Next World* (W. W. Norton & Company, 2001).

"Inosculation" was inspired by the poem "Philemon and Baucis" by Thom Gunn from *The Man with Night Sweats* (The Noonday Press, Farrar Straus Giroux, 1992).

"My Mother's Voice Echoes with Mine" is a contrapuntal poem. The italicized lines were taken directly from a letter my mother wrote me, which she presented to me on my wedding day.

Mahalo piha

My deep gratitude to the editors of the following publications in which these poems first appeared, sometimes in earlier iterations:

Belletrist: "Company"
Calyx Journal: "Ka Hale, The Nurturing Place" and "Beetmilk"
Denver Quarterly: "Makaliʻi and the Stars That Followed" and "Inosculation"
Hawaiʻi Pacific Review: "A Heart (In)Action"
Nonwhite and Woman: 131 Micro Essays on Being in the World: "When I am homesick"
ʻŌiwi, A Native Hawaiian Journal: "Ka Hale, The Nurturing Place"
Poetry Northwest: "Ghosts/ʻUhane" and "Hā"
13 Miles from Cleveland: "Memory Sonnet," "My Father's Sonnet," "My Mother's Sonnet," and "Makaliʻi and the Stars That Followed"
We the Gathered Heat: Asian American and Pacific Island Poetry, Performance, and Spoken Word: "After Her Funeral, I Dream That My Mother Tells Me Her Dreams"

Mahalo me ke aloha lā

This collection continues to be lifted by many hands, all of which I hold dearly.
I extend my sincere Mahalo nui loa…

To the communities who hold me accountable and raise their hands in praise in equal measure: Erin Armstrong, Lynne Ellis, and Rebecca Morton of Quarto; Samantha Chagollan, Saira Khan, Elizabeth Ü, and Elisabeth Vasquez Hein of Vellum; and Dawn Chen of the Tuesday Third Place Books check-in.

To the readers who cradled my earliest (and revised) words: Kristen Millares Young and Jeff and Eva Masumoto. Huge hugs to Deborah Woodard, who provided constant care and nurturing during this manuscript's infancy.

To my fellow students who hold hope for storytelling: Students in the Rainier Writing Workshop at Pacific Lutheran University; my Dear Socks and Sams in Cohort 19; and the Shapeshifter Mixies. Special shout outs to Erin Allen, Dallas Atlas, Liz Kingsley, Eric Lochridge, antmen pimentel mendoza, and Dawn Sly-Terpstra for also holding the lights that guided me during the making of this book.

To the mentors that hold the bar higher than I can reach, then teach me how to stretch: Geffrey Davis and Jennifer Elise Foerster.

To my literary ʻohana, who hold aloha ʻāina in their hearts and make room for me, too: Joe Balaz, Darlaine Māhealani Dudoit, kuʻualoha hoʻomanawanui, and Craig Santos Perez. Mahalo plenny to Misty-Lynn Sanico, whose Aloha always goes above and beyond. Deep gratitude and Aloha to Maxine Hong Kingston.

To my extended family of Native writers whose poetry holds me at my roots: Everyone at Indigenous Nations Poets, with extra special starshine on Dr. Kimberly Blaeser, Heid E. Erdrich, Halee Kirkwood, Erin Marie Lynch, Melanie Merle, Jodi Vander Molen, and Annie Wenstrup.

To those who hold space for the work to continue: Cathy Sarkowski and Heather Dwyer at The Vashon Artist Residency, where the majority of this collection was sequenced; Erin Holloway, Maura Brenin, and Katie Emerick at Storyknife Writers Retreat, where I prepared for its release; and Hugo House, where the writing was always waiting for me.

To the teachers who hold tiny seeds that flourish whenever I work with them: Rick Barot, Oliver de la Paz, Darien Hsu Gee, Jenny Johnson, Anne Liu Kellor, Brian Teare, and Jane Wong. Deep gratitude to Sandra McPherson and Bruce Snider.

To the home that welcomed this book onto its shelves: Kris Bigalk, Natasha Kane, Denise Low, and the entire Trio House family.

To my local independent bookstore, Island Books, especially bookseller extraordinaire, Lori Robinson and Knitting Book Club friends Claire Wilson-Thomas and Jennifer Wujcik. Thanks for letting me share poetry news instead of knitting projects.

To the many friends who bring boba and snacks and ask about other things besides the writing: Khristine and Erwin Angulo, Sabina Chang, Justine Gubar, Suesan Whitney Henderson, Norman Hom, Michelle Kumata, Cynthia and Bret Masterson, Michelle Ritter, Ellen and Charles Stearns, and Amanda Stoffer.

To the Gal Pal Book Club, who were open to putting poetry on the reading list: Tina Anima, Pam Dotson, Heidi Hasty, Cynthia Magoon, Kathleen Morley, Maritza Rivera, Wendy Sykes, and Jill Walzer.

To my ʻohana, who hold all the mangos: Beryl and Harding C. Parrilla, Jr., Kimberly and Lester Parrilla, Ernest Parrilla, Kiana and Nainoa Kahale, Kelia Parrilla and Sefo Pavao and Amber, Austin, Amy, and Adam Parrilla. To our beloved keiki, Loliʻi, Waikā, Ranger, Laker, and Eden. Never ending Aloha to Richard T. Schraeder and Terry Schraeder. Great big hugs to Jeanne Ocvirk. Love and Aloha to Ann Parrilla and the Kunia Parrillas, especially Henry C. Parrilla, Aileen and Roy Magno, and Virginia Keeler. Deep gratitude to Andrew McGall. And to my Waimea ʻohana, blessings to the Brighter and Perry families and their descendants.

To my children, Kupaianahahoku O kuʻuhonuahoukeolamauloa and Keahilanakilakeolamauloa, you hold every piece of my heart.

To Leia, who let me hold her leash on long neighborhood walks while I recited lines to myself and lay at my feet through most of the preparation of this collection.

To my husband, Doug, who cherishes all of my pieces every day, yet still manages to keep his hands open to the future.

And to my parents, Judith and Harding, whatever stardust you are made of, thank you for sifting it into my hands.

About the Author

Kalehua Kim is a poet living in the Pacific Northwest. Born of Hawaiian, Chinese, Filipino and Portuguese descent, her multicultural background informs much of her work. A 2023 winner of the James Welch Prize for Indigenous Poets, her poems have appeared in *Poetry Northwest*, *Denver Quarterly*, *Calyx*, and *ʻŌiwi, A Native Hawaiian Journal*.

About the Book

Mele was designed at Trio House Press through the collaboration of:

Denise Low, Lead Editor
Kris Bigalk, Supporting Editor
Natasha Kane, Interior Designer
Joel W. Coggins, Cover Designer
Shirley Cai, Author Photographer

The text is set in Adobe Caslon Pro.

About the Press

Trio House Press is an independent nonprofit press based in Minneapolis, Minnesota. We publish poetry and prose that moves, inspires, and encourages connection, empathy, and understanding, with a special emphasis on underrepresented voices and topics. To find out more about Trio House Press, please visit our website at http://www.triohousepress.org

www.ingramcontent.com/pod-product-compliance
Lightning Source LLC
Chambersburg PA
CBHW060537080526
44586CB00012B/766